Tracy Thomas

Lost and Found

Bumblebee Books
London

BUMBLEBEE PAPERBACK EDITION

A CIP catalogue record for this title is
available from the British Library.

ISBN: 978-1-83934-275-2

Bumblebee Books is an imprint of
Olympia Publishers.

First Published in 2021

Bumblebee Books
Tallis House
2 Tallis Street
London
EC4Y 0AB

Printed in Great Britain

www.olympiapublishers.com

Dedication

Chris, Callan and Caila - my rocks.
Neil - my other rock.
Hailey - my model.

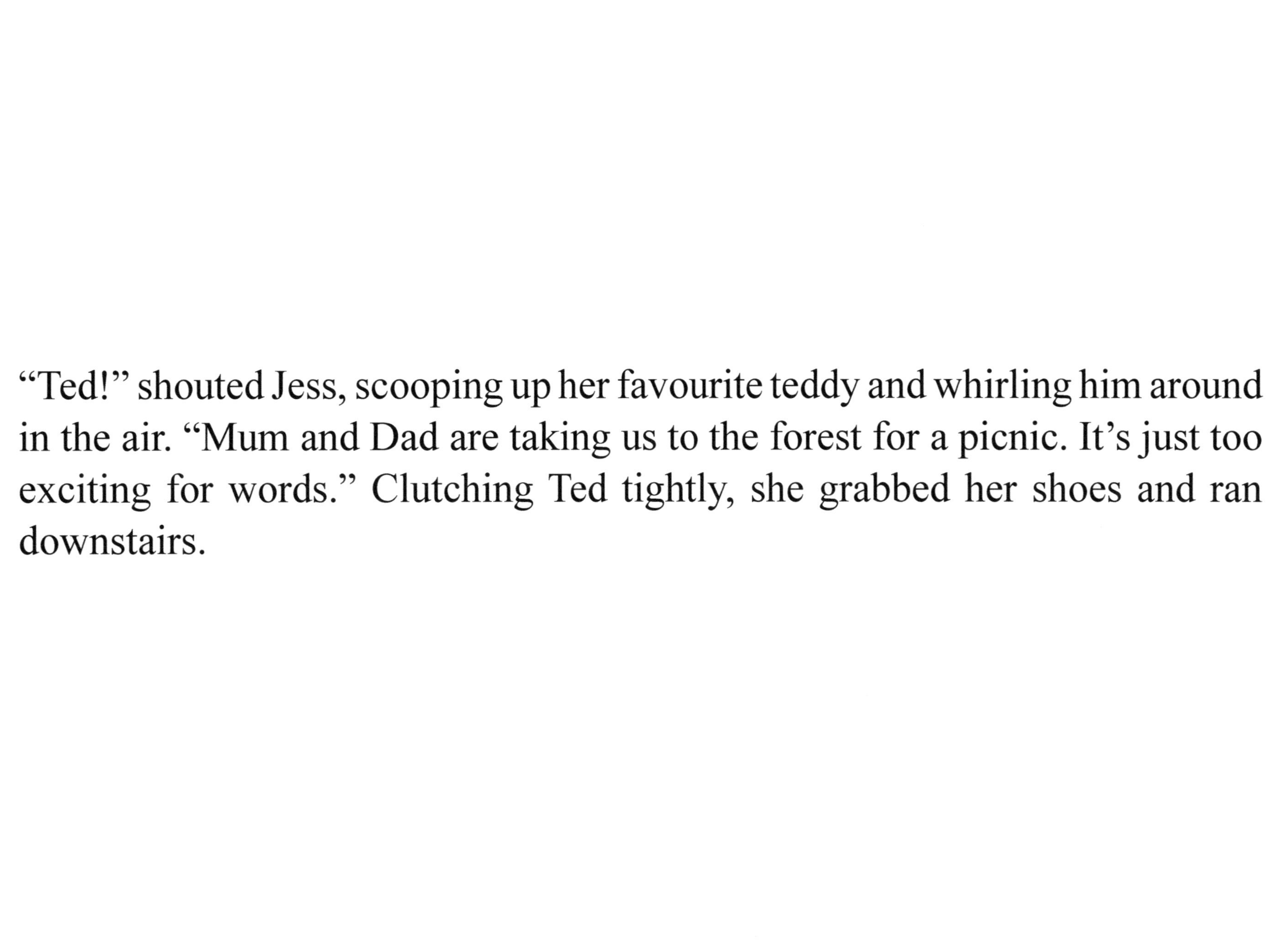

"Ted!" shouted Jess, scooping up her favourite teddy and whirling him around in the air. "Mum and Dad are taking us to the forest for a picnic. It's just too exciting for words." Clutching Ted tightly, she grabbed her shoes and ran downstairs.

"You must remember to keep very quiet," Mum said as they crossed over the bridge into the forest. "That way we might see lots of different animals."

Tall trees towered over them, butterflies hovered in the leafy canopy. Jess put her finger over Ted's mouth and whispered, "shush," in his ear.

Ted and Jess skipped ahead over the rocky path, looking up into the trees, hoping to catch a glimpse of a monkey.

"Jess," her dad called, "come and show Ted this."

Jess hurried back to where her mum and dad were staring into the undergrowth.

"What are you looking at?" asked Jess peering into the bush. Gently her dad pulled back a leaf and hidden there was a glossy, green locust. Its bright red eye looking directly at them.

"Look, Ted, look!" Jess held Ted so that he could see the little creature hiding there. "Look at his bright, red eye."

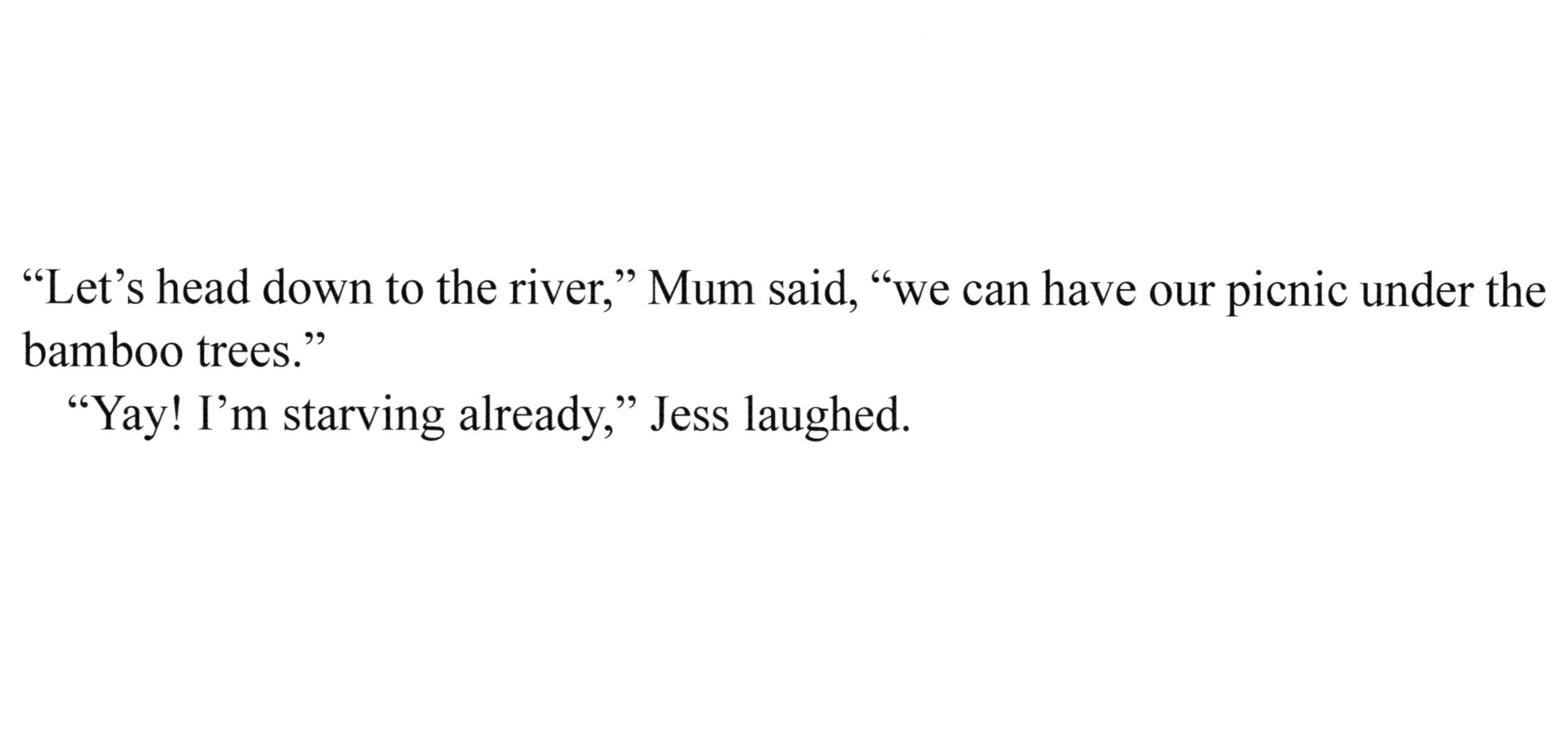

"Let's head down to the river," Mum said, "we can have our picnic under the bamboo trees."

"Yay! I'm starving already," Jess laughed.

Suddenly there was a loud, strange bark from up ahead in the trees. Branches crackled and leaves and twigs fell from the sky. The family froze in their tracks and looked up ahead to where all the commotion was coming from. A huge Sykes monkey stared down from a branch not so far ahead of them. Before they could stop her Jess ran, holding Ted above her head towards the monkey.

"Look, Ted, look!" she cried, "it's a monkey."

"Sweetie, be careful," called her mum. "Remember these are wild animals and you must keep your distance."

The monkey swiftly turned and leapt up the branch, clambering higher into the tree.

"Wow, that was awesome," said Dad, "you were lucky to get so close."

They chose a shady spot by the river, unfolding the blanket and laying out all the food. Jess just couldn't sit still though, she was so excited and rushed from one place to another. Poking the water with sticks, hopping from one rock to another, floating leaves in leaf races.

"Come and eat," Mum said, "we still have a big walk ahead of us."

Jess sat grumpily with Ted and gave him lots of snacks.

Emerging from the bamboo, a strange, big eyed creature marched away across the leafy floor.

"What's that?" Jess cried, leaping to her feet and rushing towards the animal. "Look, Ted, look!"

Her father reached down and let the chameleon climb onto his hand. "If you look carefully, Jess, you will see that his eyes move independently to each other, so he can look at me and at you at the same time. Look, he is also starting to change colour."

Ted and Jess marveled at the little green chameleon as it clung to her father's arm, slowly changing from a brilliant green to light brown. "Let's put him in the bush over there Jess, so he is safe."

"Can I hold him? Pleeeeeeease," Jess begged. Dad slowly placed the chameleon on her hand and they walked it over to the cliff where there were lots of nice places for it to climb.

They watched as the chameleon placed hand over hand and climbed a vine up the cliff. A green swallowtail butterfly landed briefly on a pink flower near them and Jess rushed off to show Ted. "Look, Ted, look," the now familiar cry.

"It's time to go, Jess, come and help us pack up," Dad shouted across the glade.

"Wait here, Ted, I won't be long," Jess murmured as she put Ted down carefully.

Jess helped her mum fold the blanket, and put some of the left-over food into the ruck sack.

"Let's go," said Dad, picking up the picnic basket. "What else do you think we will find, Jess?"

"I want to find more and more, maybe an elephant next!" Jess laughed when she saw her parent's expressions.

Skipping over to collect Ted, she noticed he was not there. "Mum, Dad, did you pick up Ted?" she asked.

"No," they both answered, glancing over to where Jess was standing.

"Where did you leave him?" Mum asked.

"Just here," Jess said, pointing to the place where Ted had been, just five minutes ago. She was starting to get very worried, but thought that maybe she had put him somewhere else. The family started carefully searching the picnic area and all the places that Jess had played.

She didn't know why she did it but she suddenly looked up, some small noise or movement had caught her attention.

High in the tree above the picnic site sat a young vervet monkey. In its arms was Ted! The monkey was holding the teddy bear close to its face and stroking the back gently.

Jess burst into tears. "Mum, Dad, there he is, that monkey has my teddy bear."

They rushed over to where Jess was standing and all looked up into the tree. The monkey was high up but holding the bear like a baby.

"Maybe it thinks it's a baby," Mum suggested.

"Maybe it doesn't have any friends," Dad suggested.

Jess wiped away some tears and looked carefully at the monkey. It really was holding Ted like a baby, gently and lovingly.

"Maybe I could give Ted to the monkey," Jess said. "Maybe it needs him more than me."

Mum and Dad looked at each other and then at Jess. "That's a lovely idea," they said. "What a kind thing to do."

"Are you sure?" Mum asked.

"Yes, I am, Ted will have such an adventure with a monkey. Imagine all the things he will see."

About the Author

Tracy Thomas lives in Kenya with her family and menagerie of animals. She was a teacher for many years and loves how stories can take children on adventures of the imagination.

Acknowledgements

Ololua forest and its flora and fauna for inspiring me in lockdown and to Caila, my lockdown forest buddy and editing champion.

www.ingramcontent.com/pod-product-compliance
Lightning Source LLC
Chambersburg PA
CBHW040714070726
47599CB00027B/862